W9-CED-025

DWAYNE JOHNSON

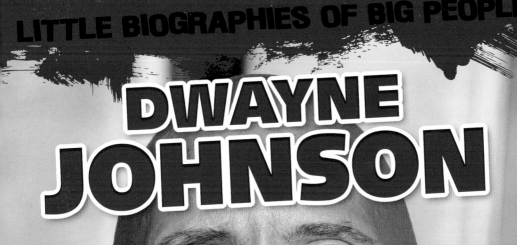

By Joan Stoltman

Gareth Stevens
PUBLISHING

Please visit our website, www.garethstevens.com. For a free color catalog of all our high-quality books, call toll free 1-800-542-2595 or fax 1-877-542-2596.

Cataloging-in-Publication Data

Names: Stoltman, Joan.
Title: Dwayne Johnson / Joan Stoltman.
Description: New York : Gareth Stevens Publishing, 2019. | Series: Little biographies of big people | Includes glossary and index.
Identifiers: ISBN 9781538232170 (pbk.) | ISBN 9781538228937 (library bound) | ISBN 9781538232187 (6 pack)
Subjects: LCSH: Johnson, Dwayne, 1972–Juvenile literature. | Wrestlers–United States--Biography–Juvenile literature. | Actors–United States–Biography–Juvenile literature.
Classification: LCC GV1196.J64 S76 2019 | DDC 796.812092 B–dc23

Published in 2019 by
Gareth Stevens Publishing
111 East 14th Street, Suite 349
New York, NY 10003

Copyright © 2019 Gareth Stevens Publishing

Designer: Tanya Dellaccio
Editor: Kate Mikoley

Photo credits: series art Yulia Glam/Shutterstock.com; cover Joe Maher/FilmMagic/ Getty Images; pp. 5, 11 Kevin Mazur/WireImage/Getty Images; p. 7 Getty Images/ Hulton Archive/Getty Images; p. 9 Collegiate Images/Getty Images; p. 13 Arnaldo Magnani/Hulton Archive/Getty Images; pp. 15, 17 Tinseltown/Shutterstock.com; p. 19 Andreas Rentz/Getty Images Entertainment/Getty Images; p. 21 Twocoms/ Shutterstock.com.

Printed in the United States of America

CPSIA compliance information: Batch #CW19GS: For further information contact Gareth Stevens, New York, New York at 1-800-542-2595.

CONTENTS

Boldface words appear in the glossary.

A Family of Wrestlers

Dwayne Johnson was born in 1972 in California. His father, Rocky, was one of the first black **wrestlers** to win the Tag Team **Championship** in World Wrestling Entertainment (WWE). Dwayne's grandfather on his mother's side was one of the first Samoan wrestlers.

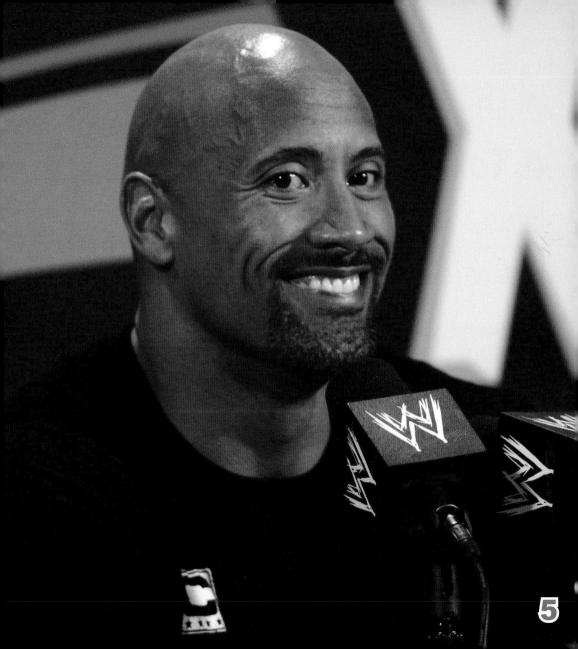

A Tough Childhood

Even though his dad was famous, Dwayne grew up poor. He moved around a lot, including to New Zealand. As a teen, Dwayne often got into trouble. He got in fights, stole things, and was even arrested.

Hard Work Pays Off

When Dwayne was 16, his life changed. His high school's football coach began **mentoring** him. His grades got better, and he started working hard to become great at football. Two years later, Dwayne was offered a spot on one of the best **college** football teams!

More Troubles

Dwayne got badly hurt several times while playing football. He became very **depressed** and even dropped out of school for a time. After college, he joined the Canadian Football League, but was cut from his team. Then he turned to the family business—wrestling.

A Champion

Dwayne decided to become a professional wrestler. He won his first championship after only a few months. He first went by the name Rocky Maivia, but soon changed this to The Rock. Dwayne won 17 pro-wrestling championships! In 2000, he wrote a best-selling book about his life.

THE ROCK SAYS...

THE MOST ELECTRIFYING MAN
IN SPORTS-ENTERTAINMENT

A Star

Five years after he began wrestling, Dwayne was asked to be on the TV show *Saturday Night Live*. He showed that he could act and be funny. Soon, Dwayne was starring in movies. He was paid more than any other actor for a first lead role!

15

Dwayne has starred in all kinds of movies, from action to **comedies**. Some of his biggest movies are *Moana* and *Jumanji: Welcome to the Jungle*. He's one of the highest paid actors today. His movies have made billions of dollars at the box office!

Working Hard

Dwayne works hard to make the most of his life. He gets up at 4 a.m. to exercise! He runs his own company that makes movies and TV shows. He also works hard to stay in touch with his fans all over the world!

Keep Pushing

Dwayne is one of the greatest wrestlers of all time. He's also one of the most successful actors in the world today! Dwayne Johnson proves that hard work can get you anywhere you want to go in life.

"I grew up where, when a door closed, a window didn't open. . . . Now the **opportunity** is here. The door is wide open."
—Dwayne Johnson

21

GLOSSARY

championship: an important competition that decides which player or team is the best in a particular sport, game, or skill

college: a school after high school

comedy: a movie, play, or book meant to make people laugh

depressed: having a serious medical condition that causes a person to feel very sad, hopeless, and unimportant

mentor: to provide advice and support to a less experienced person

opportunity: a situation in which something can be done

wrestler: someone who competes in wrestling, a sport in which two people try to throw, force, or pin each other to the ground

FOR MORE INFORMATION

BOOKS

Jones, Jen. *Dwayne Johnson*. North Mankato, MN: Capstone Press, 2017.

Kortemeier, Todd. *Superstars of WWE*. Mankato, MN: Amicus High Interest, 2017.

WEBSITES

Dwayne Johnson (The Rock) Biography
www.kidzworld.com/article/28178-dwayne-johnson-the-rock-bio
Learn more about Dwayne Johnson here.

Rocky Johnson
www.wwe.com/superstars/rockyjohnson
Read a short biography of Rocky Johnson, Dwayne Johnson's dad.

INDEX